West Yorkshire

Keith Wadd

COUNTRYSIDE BOOKS

NEWBURY BERKSHIRE

First Published 2006
© Keith Wadd, 2006

COUNTRYSIDE BOOKS
3 Catherine Road
Newbury, Berkshire

To view our complete range of books,
please visit us at
www.countrysidebooks.co.uk

ISBN 1 85306 967 1
EAN 978 1 85306 967 3

*I dedicate this book to CAMRA.
Without CAMRA's sustained efforts, good beer
might have totally vanished from Britain in the last 50 years,
and good pubs would be far more rare.*

Cover picture of Holmfirth
supplied by Bill Meadows

Photographs by the author
Designed by Peter Davies, Nautilus Design
Produced through MRM Associates Ltd, Reading
Printed by Woolnough Bookbinding Ltd., Irthlingborough

Contents

Location map   4

Introduction   5

POCKET PUB WALKS

1	Ilkley Moor *(5 or 3 miles)*	7
2	Bramhope *(8 or 5 miles)*	12
3	Harewood *(7 or 5 miles)*	17
4	Haworth *(5 miles)*	22
5	Goose Eye *(7 miles)*	27
6	Bingley *(7 or 5½ miles)*	32
7	Thorner *(6 miles)*	37
8	Fairburn Ings *(5 miles)*	42
9	Walton *(5 miles)*	47
10	Clayton West *(6 miles)*	51
11	Farnley Tyas *(4 miles)*	56
12	Holme *(5 miles)*	61
13	Triangle *(6 miles)*	66
14	Hebden Bridge *(6 miles)*	71
15	Lumbutts *(6½ miles)*	76

Area map showing location of the walks

Introduction

The main intention of this book is to show what enjoyable countryside there is in West Yorkshire and, of course, by far the best way of discovering it is on foot. The marvellous thing is that it is all virtually on the doorstep of Leeds and Bradford and the other large towns. Add to this a dense network of rights of way, plus substantial tracts of Pennine moorland to which there is now public access, and it can be appreciated that the walker in West Yorkshire is highly favoured.

The routes average around 5 miles and I have arranged them in an order that starts very appropriately I think at Ilkley Moor. The walks then go down Wharfedale, the Worth Valley, and the Aire Valley, round the lowlands in the east, then up the attractive and scarcely known southern borders close to Wakefield and Huddersfield, before finishing with three walks in the stunning scenery of Calderdale. By the time most of them have been completed, a good selection of West Yorkshire's best scenery will have been discovered or rediscovered.

Of course, the best thing of all for an enjoyable outing is good weather. Why ruin a good walk with miserable conditions? Better to leave it for another day. However, even the best of weather can sometimes turn nasty, so take a waterproof jacket and waterproof trousers with you just in case. I also recommend a pair of good boots, even in summer, and you will definitely need to wear them if you intend to walk from October to mid April. Bear in mind that some of the walks are on quite high ground so it makes sense to put an extra layer of clothing in the rucksack whatever the time of year. Even though the walks are 'short-ish', it is a good idea to bring some light refreshments, and you should always carry plenty to drink. The sketch maps for the walks are intended as a simple guide to the route, and the relevant Ordnance Survey Explorer or Outdoor Leisure map will be useful as well; hopefully it will be a good investment for many more walks.

All of the pubs sell real ale (the sort where the yeast hasn't been killed), and nearly all do hot food. At some of the pubs the food is fairly basic, though a vegetarian option is nearly always available; others offer a more upmarket and wide-ranging menu. Walkers are welcome at all of them.

Please seek prior permission if you wish to leave your car in the pub car park during the walk. However, many of the routes are easily accessible by public transport, several of them by rail: for up-to-date details phone West Yorkshire Metro at 0113 245 7676.

Happy walking – with a visit to a good pub as well!

Keith Wadd

Publisher's Note

We hope that you obtain considerable enjoyment from this book; great care has been taken in its preparation. However, changes of landlord and actual closures are sadly not uncommon. Likewise, although at the time of publication all routes followed public rights of way or permitted paths, diversion orders can be made and permissions withdrawn.

We cannot, of course, be held responsible for such diversion orders and any inaccuracies in the text which result from these or any other changes to the routes nor any damage which might result from walkers trespassing on private property. We are anxious though that all details covering the walks and pubs are kept up to date and would therefore welcome information from readers which would be relevant to future editions.

The simple sketch maps that accompany the walks in this book are based on notes made by the author whilst checking out the routes on the ground. However, for the benefit of a proper map, we do recommend that you purchase the relevant Ordnance Survey sheet covering your walk. The Ordnance Survey maps are widely available, especially through booksellers and local newsagents.

1 Ilkley Moor

The Bar t'at

Ilkley Moor is Yorkshire's best-known moor, so that alone makes a strong case for doing a walk on it. Another good reason is that it is full of interest and fine views. Ilkley Moor is the popular name for a large expanse of heather moorland that includes several moors: Rombalds Moor, Burley Moor, Ilkley Moor and others. All the moorland is urban common and access land. This walk, the longer version of which leads you up to the Twelve Apostles stone circle, visits the real Ilkley Moor, and Yorkshire purists can claim with 100% confidence that they have trodden the precise thing. Although a delight throughout the year, late July and August when the heather is in full bloom is a particularly good time for this route.

West Yorkshire

Distance – 5 miles (shorter version 3 miles).

OS Explorer 297 Lower Wharfedale and Washburn Valley. GR 117471.

Starting point Just above cattle grid, Wells Road, Ilkley.

How to get there Take the A65, which runs north-west from Leeds and Bradford to Skipton and beyond. At the main traffic lights in the middle of Ilkley, turn south up Brook Street, then at the next road junction go straight on up Wells Road. Park just above the cattle grid, either on the road or in the car park to the right. There is an excellent rail service to Ilkley from Leeds and Bradford (the station is close to the bottom of Wells Road).

THE PUB The **Bar t'at** ('baht'at' translated into English is 'without hat') on Cunliffe Road is a town centre hostelry. For anyone who likes a selection of well-kept real ales and a large menu (plus specials) of good food this is the ideal pub. Try the braised lamb shoulder with leek mash on the evening menu, or at lunchtime you could opt for the home-made beef chilli and crusty bread. The real ales are Caledonian Deuchars, Black Sheep and Taylor's Landlord, plus five guest beers. Although there is no parking at the pub, a public car park is nearby.

Lunchtime food is served from 12 noon to 2.30 pm and evening meals from 6 pm to 9 pm.
☎ *01943 608888*

1 Take the public footpath that sets off between the junction of **Wells Road** and **Crossbeck Road** immediately below the cattle grid, and go along the tarmac road. Ignore the footpath sign on

the left, and continue on a tarmac path to The Tarn, an attractive sheet of water with lots of ducks. Go either side of the lake to the steps at the far end, which soon lead to a broad path slanting up the hillside. When it forks, go left to cross the stream by a footbridge (another attractive spot), then climb the path up the hillside to the left of a belt of trees. Pause to look back for good views over **Ilkley**. Cross a broad track that leads up to the trees, and continue on a path along the foot of the rocks. Go between the **Cow** and the **Calf** and along a paved path. Turn right just before the entrance to a former quarry and clamber up the rocky slope to the top (there is no difficulty), then make for a waymark post at the far end of the quarry.

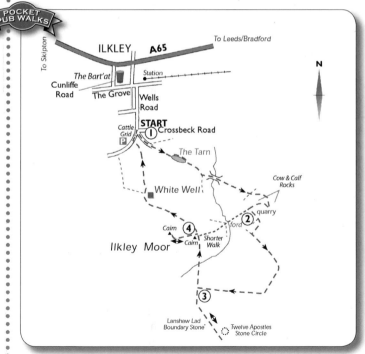

The Cow and Calf rocks above Ilkley.

2 *For the shorter walk,* go to the right of the waymark post on a broad track towards the highest point of the moor. Ford a stream, ignore side paths, and keep straight on up the hill ahead. After the top of the hill, continue in the same direction to a junction of paths by a large cairn and continue from point 4.

For the longer walk, turn left at the post on a broad path that soon leads to another waymark. Immediately after the post (but not at it), turn right on a grassy path that climbs the hillside to the right of a prominent rock. Turn left at the top of the ridge, go past a boulder (which has cup and ring marks), then along a broad track to a rock and a post on the left-hand side of the skyline. There are good views down **Lower Wharfedale**. Veer right at the rock and post, and follow the path to two more yellow posts. Turn right at the second one, which is at **Lanshaw Lass Stone**, now lying on its side in a depression, and follow a clear narrow path (at first on the top of a low bank) which keeps virtually dead straight for ½ mile.

3 Turn left when a broad, well-used track is reached. This is the
path across the moor to **Ilkley** from **Dick Hudson's**, a popular
pub near **Eldwick**. Continue to the top of the hillside to the left
of the **Lanshaw Lad boundary stone** and on the left a few
yards further is the **Twelve Apostles stone circle**. Now retrace
your steps and at point 3 keep straight on until you reach a
junction of paths by a cairn and a stunning view of **Ilkley**.

4 Turn left up a path (*those on the shorter walk, keep straight on*)
for 300 yards to reach a cairn on the real **Ilkley Moor**. The
view is outstanding; the **Bowland Hills** are on the left, ahead
you can see over **Ilkley** and up **Wharfedale**, then, round to the
right, the **North Yorkshire Moors**, the **Yorkshire Wolds** and,
if it is very clear, the **Lincolnshire Wolds**. Retrace your steps
to the main path, turn left and descend a steep rocky path to
the white-painted building of **White Wells**. The discovery in the
1700s of the pure water here eventually led to the development
of Ilkley as a spa town. One of the original baths at White Wells
can be visited and there is a brief history on the adjacent display
boards (plus refreshments next door). After this pause, follow
one of the paths down the hillside to the cattle grid where the
walk started, and then you can walk down to the **Bar t'at** in the
middle of **Ilkley**.

Places of interest nearby

   Ilkley is a spacious small town with pleasant streets. The
parish church is on the site of the Roman fort (Olicana),
which was on a junction of Roman roads. It has a 13th-
century doorway and Saxon crosses in the churchyard.
Next door to the church is the 16th-century manor house,
now an interesting local museum.
☎ *01943 600066*

2 **Bramhope**

The Fox & Hounds

Bramhope, where this walk begins, is full of interest. The route is only a mile or two from the northern outskirts of Leeds, but for much of the time you would think you were deep in rural England. It is a pleasant mixture of woodland and meadow, with several stretches of attractive green lane, and there are frequent outstanding views. On the longer walk that takes you to the Arthington road north-east of Bramhope, there is a good chance of seeing red kites, which were recently introduced at nearby Harewood. This circuit then loops back towards the village via the railway bridges that were part of the former Arthington junction on the line to Otley. From here it joins the shorter route at the delightfully named Staircase Lane.

THE PUB The **Fox & Hounds**, which dates from the 1800s, is a village pub that also caters for people from further afield. Yorkshire cricket enthusiasts may have a nostalgic drool over a photograph in the corridor by the Gents. There is an extensive menu of main courses, plus a specials board. The real ales are Black Sheep, Cropton and Taylor's, plus a guest beer.

Food is available from 11.30 am to 8.45 pm on Monday to Saturday and from 12 noon to 7.45 pm on Sundays.
☎ *0113 284 2448*

1 On leaving the **Fox & Hounds** turn left down the road marked 'Otley' on the large metal signpost at the top of the splendid village cross. The road soon joins the main A660 at the bottom of the hill by the parish church. Cross the road to a bridleway sign, then turn left up the A660 towards Otley. Note the Puritan Chapel on the right built in 1649 during Cromwell's protectorate.

For the shorter walk, carry on along the main road for a few yards, then slant right down **Staircase Lane** until you reach point 5.

Distance – 8 miles (shorter version 5 miles).

OS Explorer 297 Lower Wharfedale and Washburn Valley. GR 248433.

Starting point The Fox & Hounds at Bramhope.

How to get there *The Fox & Hounds is at the crossroads in the middle of Bramhope village. Take the A660 from Leeds, and turn left into Bramhope village just before the Holiday Inn is reached on the right. From Bradford take the A658, then the second turn right after the airport roundabout. There is a frequent bus service from Leeds.*

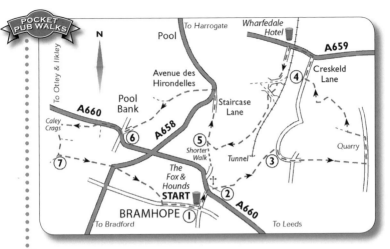

2 *For the longer walk*, retrace your steps briefly, then turn left down the bridleway. Turn left when a road of houses is reached, then left down a path after **No. 34**. The clearly signposted path crosses two more roads in the housing estate, enters a wood, then comes to a green lane.

3 Turn right when the lane reaches a road and, where it bends sharply right, keep straight on along the bridleway. Continue in the same direction through fields, keeping close by the ditch on the right. The path enters a green lane with a deep gritstone quarry (still working) on the left. Turn left along the road at the end, then immediately after the quarry entrance, go left along an attractive green lane. Go over a stile on the right immediately before two fine yew trees and descend the hillside keeping the wall on the left. I saw red kites here. Slant left close to the edge of the wood, cross the corner of a field to a gate in the wall, and then, almost immediately, another gate. Turn sharp left alongside the wood, then sharp right after you enter the next field. Go over a stile by a ruined barn and slant across a short field to **Creskeld Lane**.

4 Turn right and down the lane, then left for a short distance along the pavement of the A659. Immediately after the railway bridge, turn left up an unmetalled lane. Go under a former railway bridge, bear right when the lane forks, then go under another railway bridge. Bear left after the second bridge and follow the track close to the Leeds–Harrogate line (still in frequent use).

The path slants to the right up a green valley. Go to the left of the gate at the top and through a kissing gate into an enclosed path and then a field. Ignore the stile, and slant across the next field to the right of **Staircase House**, then over a stone stile to **Staircase Lane**.

5 Turn right and down the lane between tall hedges. Continue straight on at the bottom of the hill (though the 'alternative path' on the left may be taken), then turn right briefly on reaching the A658. Turn left under the '**Avenue des Hirondelles**' archway and walk up the avenue. Veer slightly right on entering a field. Bear left just inside the wood (not through a gap in an old railway embankment), go past rocks on the left, then up a steep bank to the right. Continue through wooded old quarry workings,

The Arthington Viaduct and Almscliff Crag viewed from the walk.

and immediately to the left of stone terrace houses and garages. Drop down to an unmetalled road, then continue past houses on the left to the main A660.

6 Turn right, cross a minor road (Old Pool Bank), and go along the A660 with fine views to the right. Cross the A660 at the end of the housing on the left, then take the right-hand of the two tracks and go between two houses into a wood. The path goes beside a fence on the left, then climbs a rocky hillside. Shortly after two lines of wooden pylons leave the path to visit the precipitous edge of **Caley Crags**. There are fine views over **Wharfedale**. Now turn sharp left on a broad track that goes through a kissing gate (ignore the path to **Quarry Farm Road** immediately after) and continue in the same direction through the woodland of **Caley Deer Park**.

7 Turn left at the footpath sign at the top, along the path to **Pool Bank Road**. The path soon leaves the wood (via the stile at the right-hand corner). Keep to the top of the field, then follow the green lane to the A658. Cross the road to a path that goes between the houses and soon leads into fields. Slant right after a stile by a large stone gatepost, then follow a ruined wall on the right to a stile and a walled path. Turn left along the road (**Old Lane**) and into **Bramhope**.

Places of interest nearby

Otley, two miles away, is an attractive and lively market town. In its churchyard (approached along Church Lane) is an impressive monument to the 23 workers who were killed in the construction of Bramhope Tunnel. Thomas Chippendale, the famous 18th-century furniture maker, was born in Otley and there is a statue of him in Manor Square.

3 Harewood

The Harewood Arms Hotel

This walk provides an excellent example of the fine countryside on Leeds' doorstep, less than three miles from the outskirts of the city. Much of the route is in the parkland and woodland of Harewood Park, and there is a stretch beside the River Wharfe if you opt for the full circuit. The walk also visits Harewood church in its delightful setting. You will almost certainly see deer along the way, there is a good chance of spotting red kites (very large birds with forked anvil tails), and there are many attractive views of Lower Wharfedale. The last part of the walk, in woodland to the west of the main road, is on the Wallside Permissive Path that can occasionally be closed. (☎ *0113 2886252 to check*).

West Yorkshire

Distance – 7 miles (shorter version 5 miles).

OS Explorer 297 Lower Wharfedale and Washburn Valley or 289 Leeds. GR 322452.

Starting point The Harewood Arms Hotel at Harewood.

How to get there *Harewood is on the A61 between Leeds and Harrogate. The Harewood Arms is on the east side of the road, just north of the traffic lights. There is an excellent bus service to Harewood from Leeds (No 36 to Ripon) every 20 minutes.*

THE PUB The **Harewood Arms Hotel** is an atmospheric old coaching inn dating back to 1815 and still retains its stables. As well as the restaurant menu, there is an extensive bar menu, also a specials board that is changed daily. Try the Yorkshire rarebit, or the baked rainbow trout. The real ales are Sam Smith's. The hotel is residential, and has 24 bedrooms.

Bar meals are served from 12 noon till 2.30 pm and 5.30 pm till 8.30 pm on Monday to Friday and 12 noon to 8.30 pm at weekends. Restaurant meals are served every evening from 7 pm to 8.30 pm and also from 12 noon to 2 pm on Sundays.
☎ *0113 288 6566*

1 Cross the main A61 road after leaving the Harewood Arms and turn right, then left along **Church Lane**. *For the shorter walk, when the lane becomes walled, continue straight on to point 3. For the full route,* turn right just before the road becomes walled along a broad grassed path that soon leads to **Bondgate**, an attractive village street. At the end of Bondgate, turn left along the A61 for 200 yards or so, then when the main road begins to

swing left, turn right onto a farm track by a concealed **Ebor Way** signpost. The track becomes an enjoyable hedged lane down the hillside. Turn left when the **River Wharfe** is reached and continue along the broad track close to the river. Turn right just before a low stone chimney, go through a farm gate and continue along a track close to the river. Look left to see the tower of **Harewood Castle** (not open to the public) poking out of the trees, and ahead the splendid arches of **Harewood Bridge** soon come into view. Just before the bridge, go down almost to the river on a faint path which goes to the right of a clump of trees then climbs up steps to the A61.

2 Turn left along the A61 to the road junction (take special care at the corner), then go on a path signposted to **Church Lane** through tall wooden gates with lions' faces. Just after the house, you may see deer in the field on the left. The waymarked path goes straight ahead up the steep hillside.

Harewood Bridge over the Wharfe.

3 Turn left at the top, over the cattle grid, then immediately turn right and along a broad lane to **Harewood church**. This is a delight to visit, both for its attractive setting and its 15th- and 16th-century richly decorated alabaster tombs, which are amongst the best in England.

Retrace your steps, cross the cattle grid, then continue along a tarmac estate road (the continuation of **Church Lane**). There are good views on this stretch: first **Almscliff Crag** and the **lower Washburn Valley** on the right, then **Arthington Viaduct** with **Ilkley Moor** beyond, then the hillside of **Otley Chevin** as the view continues to unfold. Turn left at the

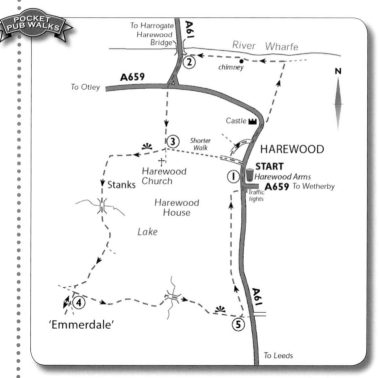

junction of bridleways with a notice saying 'Private Road to Stank'. Keep straight on when **Stank** is reached, through a gate marked 'bridleway', then over a bridge across a stream. Keep straight on at the junction of estate tracks immediately after. The track climbs by a wood on the left, then descends to a gate with a magnificent willow on the right. Follow the bridleway sign, and keep in parkland close to the wood on the right. Glance back for a view of **Harewood House** and lake. Go to the right of buildings and into a wood, climbing quite steeply. After the path turns right, fork left up a sunken path to a junction of paths.

4 Keep straight on for a short distance to view on the left where the TV series *Emmerdale Farm* is filmed, then retrace your steps to the junction of paths. Turn right and follow a broad track that continues through woodland for two-thirds of a mile. There is no danger of taking a wrong turn as any wrong turn will say 'Private No Entry'. Just after an ornate bridge, the path re-enters parkland and climbs steadily. Towards the top there are good views of **Harewood House** on the left.

5 Just before the path comes out on to the A61, turn left along a path by a notice saying 'The Wallside Permissive Path'. This goes through attractive mature woodland for over a mile before joining the A61, where you turn left into **Harewood village**.

Places of interest nearby

Harewood House is an imposing 18th-century mansion designed by John Carr with interiors by Robert Adam. There is Chippendale furniture, paintings by J M W Turner and El Greco, and regularly changing exhibitions. The gardens were laid out by Capability Brown.
☎ 0113 218 1000

The Old White Lion Hotel

Haworth and the Brontë Moors are a celebrated Yorkshire place. The walk is almost entirely a moorland one, and gives a good flavour of the countryside in which Emily Brontë's *Wuthering Heights* was located. These moors were also a major focus of the recent Right to Roam campaign. Much of the route is on broad tracks and paths, but, in places, narrower moorland paths are used, though these are easily followed. The descent to Brontë Bridge beside the Brontë Falls is dramatic (it also needs care!). The views are good, though not wide-ranging, and I always enjoy the sharp contrast between the moorland and the green fields. This is a particularly appropriate walk for late summer when the heather is in full flush, and it smells so nice too!

THE PUB

The **Old White Lion Hotel** at the top of Main Street in Haworth is 300 years old. It is a former coaching inn, and has not been too much altered. These days it has 14 residential rooms There is an extensive bar menu: try the steak and kidney pudding or the sea bass fillet. A venison casserole was on the specials board on the day of my visit. The real ales are Tetley's and Theakston's.

Bar food is served from 11.30 am to 2.30 pm and 6 pm to 9 pm on Monday to Friday and 12 noon till 9.30 pm on Saturday and Sunday. The restaurant opens from 7 pm to 9.30 pm every day and also from 12 noon till 2.30 pm on Sundays.
☎ *01535 646222*

1 Leave the car park by a path on the left-hand side, which leads to the main street in **Haworth village**. Turn right at the church on a path signposted to **Penistone Hill**. The path goes between iron

Distance – 5 miles.

OS Explorer Outdoor Leisure 21 South Pennines. GR 029373.

Starting point Car park at Brontë Parsonage Museum (pay and display).

How to get there *Turn off the A629 Keighley to Halifax road at Cross Hills, 2½ miles south of Keighley. Haworth is a mile further on along the A6033, then the B6142. Continue along the B6142 to the top of the village then turn left at the 'Brontë Parsonage Museum' sign. There are frequent buses from Keighley, or you can arrive by train on the Worth Valley line, perhaps pulled by a steam engine.*

The delightful Brontë Bridge near the falls.

railings at the bottom of the churchyard, then continues as an enclosed path along the hillside. Keep straight on at the junction of paths and follow the **Brontë Way**, signposted to **Oxenhope**, along an enjoyable narrow walled path. Turn sharp left at the stile into the field and follow the wall on the left to a stile by a lamppost where you leave the **Brontë Way**.

[2] Turn right and follow the tarmac lane up the hill to **Dimples Lane**. Turn left, then almost immediately turn right and onto a moorland track. You are now on **Penistone Hill**, a popular moorland 'urban common' crossed by a plethora of tracks and paths. When the track narrows to a path, keep close to the wall at the left by the edge of the moor. Take the path signposted '**Brontë Falls, Top Withins**' close to a grassed-over quarry on the right. Keep to the left of a car park and continue by the wall on the left past houses and buildings.

3 Briefly turn left when the road is reached, but almost immediately turn right on the access road to **Drop Farm Tearoom**, signposted to **Brontë Falls** and **Top Withins**. Continue on a pleasant moorland path after **Drop Farm**, keeping a wall on the left. There are good views leftwards to **Ovenden Moor** (with the windfarm), and **Stairs Lane**, which climbs the hillside beyond **Leeshaw Reservoir**.

4 Leave the wall at a footpath sign and follow the path signposted to **Brontë Falls** and **Top Withins**, which slants right across the moor. It is narrow but clear, and dead straight. Turn left when a broad, crushed-stone track is reached and follow it for almost a third of a mile until, at a footpath sign just before **Harbour Lodge,** a path goes off on the right. Ignore the **Top Withins** route that soon goes off on the left, and follow the moorland path close to a stream. Quite suddenly, it drops steeply to **Brontë Bridge** with the **Brontë Falls** on the right. The descent needs care, and don't be afraid to use your hands. For a full frontal of the lower cataract, impressive when in spate, wander cautiously to the right.

5 **Brontë Bridge** is a stone clapper bridge in a delightful situation. **Top Withins**, popularly regarded (though informed opinion

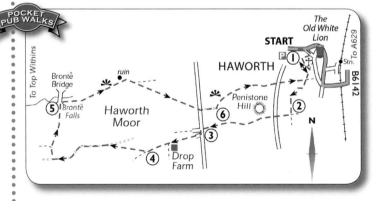

refutes it) as the Wuthering Heights of Emily Brontë's novel is a mile further on. *If you wish to visit Top Withins* (which adds 2 miles to the walk), cross the bridge, climb up the steep hillside, then turn left up the valley. *To continue the main walk,* turn right at **Brontë Bridge** and follow the broad rocky path at the right-hand side of the valley. There are good views down the **Worth Valley** with **Ilkley Moor** in the distance. After about two thirds of a mile, you come to a ruined building on the left and, 100 yards after, slant right and across the moor on a clear path. After ½ mile, go through a kissing gate, cross a road and continue straight on along a broad stony track used as a car park.

6 After 100 yards, turn left on a path signposted to **Haworth** and **Moorside car park**. Glance back for good views of the moors beyond **Top Withins**. The broad path passes the actual **Penistone Hill** on the right and descends towards a belt of trees. Go straight across the road and down a walled lane. When the avenue of sycamores comes out at a junction of paths, turn left and retrace your steps to **Haworth**. Turn left on entering the churchyard, then go left up a lane that leads to the car park via the **Brontë Parsonage Museum**, which is well worth a visit.

Places of interest nearby

The Brontë sisters lived at Haworth Parsonage for most of their short lives, and the informative and unpretentious **Parsonage Museum** is full of Brontë memorabilia. The museum is open from 10 am to 5.30 pm April to September, and 11 am to 5 pm October to March.
☎ *01535 642323.*

5 **Goose Eye**

The Turkey Inn

This is a fine Pennine walk just beyond the outskirts of Keighley. There are upland meadows as well as airy moorland and the wooded valley of Newsholme Dean, which you enter within a few yards of leaving the hamlet of Goose Eye. From the moors you will have splendid views of the surrounding countryside, and at one point you can see towards Top Withins and the Brontë Moors. Although glorious all year, the months of April and May when Newsholme Dean is full of spring flowers and the curlews are back on the moors are specially recommended for this walk. If you don't have time for the full circuit, just do the first bit up Newsholme Dean – you'll love it!

THE PUB The **Turkey Inn** is a 200 year old village pub with low ceilings, and real fires in winter. It brews its own beer, Turkey Bitter, and its other real ales are Tetley's and Abbot, plus two guest beers. Try the oven-roasted duck, the Whitby scampi or the home-made steak and ale pie.

Meals are available from 12 noon to 2 pm and 6.15 pm to 9 pm (12 noon to 7 pm on Sundays). The Turkey is closed all day on Mondays and at lunchtime on Tuesdays.
☎ *01535 681339*

1 Turn right on leaving the **Turkey** (left from the pub car park). When the road bends left, go straight on through a stone gap stile by a footpath sign and cross a footbridge over **Dean Beck**. Continue on the path up the wooded valley, keeping the

Distance – 7 miles.

OS Explorer Outdoor Leisure 21 South Pennines. GR 029405.

Starting point The Turkey Inn, Goose Eye.

How to get there *From Keighley, take the B6143 towards Oakworth, then go right almost immediately up West Lane. After two thirds of a mile turn left along Braithwaite Road, signposted to Laycock. A few yards after Laycock, turn left down a steep hill to Goose Eye. There is a frequent bus service from Keighley bus station to Laycock (½ mile from Goose Eye).*

The clapper bridge in Newsholme Dean.

stream on the left. Keep to the right of the millpond, ignoring a path going down to a footbridge over the stream and across a footbridge. The path then enters a walled section before meeting an unmetalled road.

2 Turn left down the road, and then bear left after the last house down a green lane, which crosses **Dean Beck** by a splendid clapper bridge. Continue straight on to a gate, then go slightly left up the hillside and into a narrow wooded valley. After the trees end, strike left up the valley side to a step stile and gate. Continue along an enclosed path with views on the left to nearby **Keighley**, then turn sharp right along a walled lane.

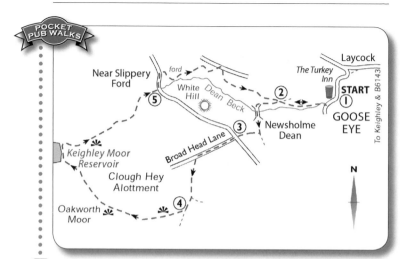

POCKET PUB WALKS

Laycock

Near Slippery Ford

ford

The Turkey Inn

White Hill

Dean Beck

START
①

GOOSE EYE

⑤

②

To Keighley & B6143

③

Newsholme Dean

Broad Head Lane

Keighley Moor Reservoir

Clough Hey Alottment

④

Oakworth Moor

N

3 *If you want a shorter walk,* though it is not recommended as it involves a mile of road walking, turn right along the metalled road to rejoin the main route at point 5. Otherwise, cross the road and go along **Broad Head Lane**, a pleasant cul de sac with wide verges. Turn left at a public bridleway sign (just before the 'private road' notice), and continue straight on, through a gate and up a field by a wall on the left. Veer right at the top, ignoring the gate, and keep the wall on the left.

4 Don't cross the stile into the next field, but turn right to a step stile in the field corner. There are good views from here, particularly to the north. The path now keeps close to the wall on the left for more than ½ mile (NB: the wall becomes tumbledown for a while when the path enters moorland and goes to the right of a plantation of Scots pines). This is enjoyable moorland walking. Soon after the pines, the path goes through the wall and then keeps it on the right. The prospect opens up to the left now, and there are good views over the upper end of the **Worth Valley** to the **Brontë Moors** and **Boulsworth Hill**. The tributary valley behind the Worth Valley is **Ponden Clough**

leading to **Ponden Kirk**, and in the valley beyond this are the **Brontë Falls** and **Top Withins**.

The clear path eventually leaves the wall behind and continues across the moorland to **Keighley Moor Reservoir**. If you like moorland, this is a splendid place, and you feel that you are miles from anywhere. Go along the dam, then turn right and down the reservoir road, with good views into **Newsholme Dean** straight ahead.

5 Turn left when the road is reached, then shortly afterwards turn right through the farmyard of **Slitheroford Farm**. Turn right after the gate and round the edge of the field to a gate and a ford (which can sometimes be quite high). I don't know whether this is the actual **Near Slippery Ford** (there is also a Far Slippery Ford), but it is a charming rural scene. Follow the pylons up the hillside to a gap in the wall, then keep slightly to the right of the pylons to a step stile, then to an ingenious stile on a boulder in the wall, then a stile by a gate. The path continues in the same direction with good views into **Newsholme Dean**. It then goes over a step stile, and immediately to the left of a barn and a farmhouse, before continuing up the farm access road to **Todley Hall Road**. After a few yards turn right at a public bridleway sign, and follow a heather-fringed green lane down into the valley. Keep straight on when you cross an unmetalled road after ½ mile, and retrace your steps to the **Turkey** along the attractive path you started out on earlier.

Places of interest nearby

East Riddlesden Hall is a National Trust property, and is on Bradford Road, a mile from Keighley town centre. It is a fine example of a 17th-century manor house, and also has a celebrated garden.

☎ 01909 511061 for details of opening times.

6 Bingley

The Brown Cow

Bingley is a pleasant commuter town with an attractive parish church. The prominent large chimney of Damart is a reminder of its long-time connection with textiles. This is an attractive well-wooded walk, and there are also rocky outcrops and a stretch alongside the River Aire. The route leads into the St Ives Estate, which formerly belonged to the Ferrand family who transformed Harden Grange, once a Cistercian monastic grange, into the St Ives mansion. The circuit is full of good views, and at one point on the longer walk the whole of Bingley is at your feet. This really is a ramble on the doorstep of a large city, but unless you knew, you would hardly guess that the centre of Bradford is a mere 6 miles away.

Distance – 7 miles (shorter version 5½ miles)

OS Explorer 288 Bradford and Huddersfield. GR 105393.

Starting point The Brown Cow, Ireland Bridge, Bingley.

How to get there *Turn off the A650 Bradford to Keighley road and make your way into the centre of Bingley on the B6265. Just north of the central traffic lights, turn south-west along Millgate (B6429). The Brown Cow is on the left immediately after the bridge over the river. There are frequent rail and bus services to Bingley, and the railway station is centrally placed.*

THE PUB

The **Brown Cow** has deservedly been a popular pub for many years. There is a wide-ranging menu of meals and snacks, including several vegetarian dishes. Look out for the chicken, ham and mushroom pie and the sole stuffed with crab. There are four Taylor's real ales, plus guest beers.

Meals are served from 12 noon to 2.15 pm (2.45 pm on Sundays) and 6 pm to 8.45 pm.
☎ *01274 569482*

1 Turn right on leaving the **Brown Cow** and cross the bridge over the **Aire**. Immediately after the bridge, turn right along '**Riverside Walk**' down to **Myrtle Park**. Cross the **Aire** by a metal bridge and continue up the steps ahead. Turn left after the steps (don't go up the next flight) and continue through woodland with the river far below. Turn right just before a house on an enclosed path that leads into a field and then to a lane.

2 Turn left along the lane, then turn right immediately after the houses down steps and over a narrow stone bridge. Continue in

the same direction across the golf course and follow a path clearly marked by white stones. The path then crosses the corner of a meadow (note the fine beech in the wood on the left), and enters **Ruin Bank Wood**. Go up the rocky path, turn right briefly when it joins another path, then continue up wooded hillside by a fence on the left. The path then slants across two meadows with fine stone gap stiles, enters a walled section, then follows a wall on the right to a road. Go left briefly, then through a stile on the right marked '**MW**' (for Millennium Way). Now follow a faint path by the wall on the right across several fields with wide views.

3 At the T-junction of paths, turn right and keep to the top of the wood. The path fairly soon descends steeply through birches to join a broad rutted track. Just before a house, turn left (stile

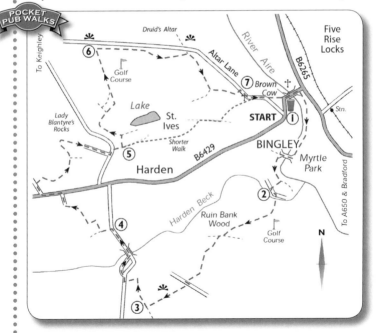

indistinct) along the bottom of
a field, cross the **Wilsden Beck**
by stepping stones and climb
up to the road. Turn right past
the garden centre and keep
straight on down **Mill Hill Top**.
Turn left at the bottom over the
bridge across the **Harden Beck**
and walk up the road as far as a
public footpath sign on the left,
shortly after a roadside seat.

Lady Blantyre sitting by her rock.

4 This part of the route has some
muddy places and, in winter
and wet weather, it can be avoided by continuing up the road
into **Harden**, then turning left, then right up the **Keighley road**
and right into the St Ives estate to reach point 5. *For the full, fair
weather walk*, shortly after the roadside seat, turn left at a footpath
sign and, after 200 hundred yards, go through a wooden gap
stile on the right. In the second field go through a stile on the
left, then through a gap stile on the right. Slant across the field
towards the second house on the left then follow an enclosed path
to a lane leading to the **Cullingworth road**. Turn left, then turn
right shortly afterwards up **Ryecroft Road**. At the first bend, turn
right along an enclosed footpath and, when fields are reached,
keep to the right close to the houses. Cross an access road to a
stile, slant across two fields to rejoin the access road and continue
past a house on the right. Take the footpath that goes to the right
of the house ahead, then cross a field to a lane. The lane swings
right and soon leads to a long row of stone terrace housing (**Moor
Edge**). Turn left at the end onto the **Keighley road**, then through
an imposing gateway on the right into the **St Ives estate**.

5 *For the shorter walk*, continue along the tarmac road after the
display board, then turn right at a footpath sign just after a
small car park and picnic tables. The path keeps to the top of

woodland and passes the **St Ives mansion**. Turn right when a tarmac road is reached (note the fine yew just before), then left onto a footpath into woodland immediately after a stone house. Turn left at a footpath sign shortly afterwards, then keep close to the wall on the left for a third of a mile to reach **Altar Lane**. Turn right, and follow directions in point 7.

For the main walk, shortly after entering the grounds, turn left at the display board and walk long the '**red path**'. Turn left at a T-junction, and continue along the 'red path' as it climbs steadily through the trees past **Lady Blantyre's Rock** ('the dowager was accustomed in summer to sit underneath this rock reading and enjoying the scenery'). The path continues past a heather moor on the left and across **St Ives golf course**.

6 Turn right on an attractive path through mature woodland with Scots pines. Turn left after a kissing gate and go along the path signposted '**Druids Altar**' for about 300 yards. The altar in a clump of gritstone rocks is scarcely impressive, but the view of **Bingley** at your feet is stunning. Retrace your steps and go past the kissing gate and along a walled lane. Immediately after a stone building turn left down a steep lane.

7 Turn right on reaching **Altar Lane**, which descends steeply. It passes a large pylon on the left, then narrows and bends right. Turn left here (there are stone steps) down a wooded path that leads out opposite the **Brown Cow**.

Places of interest nearby

Five Rise Locks, a flight of five locks on the Leeds and Liverpool Canal, is a famous piece of 18th-century canal engineering, and the nearby **Three Rise Locks** are also impressive. They are a short walk along the towpath from Bingley town centre.

7 **Thorner**

The Mexborough Arms

The **countryside around Thorner** is a good example of the richly varied nature of West Yorkshire's landscape. This part is more reminiscent of the Home Counties than the north of England. It is well wooded and makes very agreeable walking. The first part of the route is on magnesian limestone and the latter part on gritstone. The substantial bastions of Hetchell Crags come as a surprise when they appear through the trees. Stone for York Minster was quarried near Thorner. I do not know the precise location, though the walk passes a grassed-over quarry. The walk is on easy-to-follow paths and goes through several attractive woods. There is lots of birdlife, including four species of tit, skylarks, yellowhammers, woodpeckers and the ubiquitous pheasant.

Distance – 6 miles.

OS Explorer 289 Leeds. GR 378404.

Starting point The Mexborough Arms, Main Street, Thorner.

How to get there *Thorner lies north-east of Leeds between the A64 and the A58 roads. Approaching from Leeds, take the A64 towards York. Shortly after leaving the outskirts of Leeds, turn left along Thorner Lane to Thorner. There is also a frequent bus service from Leeds to Thorner.*

THE PUB The **Mexborough Arms** in Thorner is an unpretentious village pub with an attractive beer garden overlooking the bowling green and a welcoming fire in winter. Try the steak and ale pie or the corned beef hash with giant Yorkshire pudding. The real ales are John Smith's and Tetley.

Food is served from 12 noon to 10 pm (Easter to October) and 3 pm to 10 pm in the winter (from 12 noon at weekends).
☎ *01132 892316*

1 Turn left on leaving the **Mexborough Arms** and walk along Thorner's pleasant **Main Street** towards the church tower. **St Peter's**, which is mainly Victorian apart from its ancient tower, is built of limestone and this contrasts with the gritstone of most of the nearby houses. After leaving the churchyard, continue along the road, then turn left along **Milner Lane** (signposted to **Scarcroft** and **Bardsey**). Not long after the speed derestriction signs, take the footpath on the right signposted '**Wothersome via Jubilee Bridge**'. Keep well left, close to the hedge in the first field, then continue in the same direction in the second field along the side of an attractive valley. The path enters **Milner**

Wood, and bears left down to the stream, which it crosses by the **Jubilee Bridge**. The path soon leaves the wood and goes up a field close to a hedge on the left. Turn right at the top along **Kennels Lane**, and continue along it till it peters out after about ½ mile. There are no kennels, but if you hear the thud of hoofs they are on the gallops over the hedge on the left.

2 Ignore the bridleway to the left and go through a gap in the hedge on the right, then down a field by the hedge on the right. Bear left along an enjoyable path in attractive mixed woodland (**Ragdale Plantation**), and resist all temptations to cross the stream. Turn left when the path, still in woodland, reaches a T-junction of bridleways. At the next junction of paths (by a tumbledown wall) turn right for a few yards, and then left along a bridleway which runs just inside a wood with a field close by on the right. The path eventually enters the field and keeps close to a hedge on the left. For the last 200 yards before it crosses

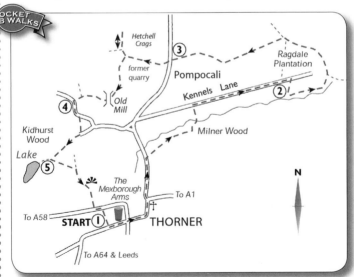

The church of St Peter in Thorner.

the Thorner to Bardsey road at **Pompocali**, the path is on the course of a Roman road. Pompocali, apart from its name, is without interest.

3 Continue down a pleasant lane with **Hetchell Wood** on the right. Just before a ford is reached, go through a kissing gate on the right. The gritstone crags of **Hetchell Crags** are straight ahead. After the rocks have been suitably explored, retrace your steps to the kissing gate, go left for a few yards, then over the stile on the right. The path keeps fairly close to the stream on the right in attractive surroundings, and at one point goes round a large crag. Beyond the hillside on the left is a grassed-over quarry. Go over a wooden step stile by a gate, past the ruins of a former

mill, and under a stout stone bridge of the former Wetherby to Leeds railway. Continue along a pleasant green lane and go through a gate into a field by a waymark. The path swings left and returns to the lane by a gate close to a horse chestnut tree. Continue along the lane, and ignore the stile on the right.

4 Turn left when the road is reached and walk along it for ¼ mile to a public footpath sign on the right. The path climbs up the hillside to the immediate right-hand side of the farm building at the top, then goes through two gates to a lane. Turn right and, when the lane goes into woodland, ignore the path on the left by the wall. Fairly soon, an attractive lake with an appropriately placed seat is reached.

5 Retrace your steps for 200 yards, then go through a kissing gate on the right between two hollies. Strike diagonally across the field (just to the left of the right-hand pylon) and in the same direction over the next field. Pause to look at the view (it's the best viewpoint on the walk) and walk down a green lane with pleasant views of **Thorner** ahead. Turn left along the road past the former Methodist church (now apartments), then turn right immediately afterwards down an enclosed footpath that leads into Thorner's **Main Street** opposite the **Fox**. Turn left for a short distance to the **Mexborough Arms**.

Places of interest nearby

Bramham Park is an impressive 18th-century mansion three miles east of Thorner. The house owes much to French influences, and the gardens are a celebrated example of the French-style formal gardening of the time. The house is open only to groups by special arrangement, but the gardens are open daily from April to September.
☎ *01937 846000.*

The White Horse

This walk visits the Fairburn Ings RSPB Reserve, a charming blend of wetland and woodland, not only good for birds, but in the summer for butterflies, dragonflies and wild flowers. This is former coal mining country, and the lakes and wetlands of Fairburn were caused by mining subsidence. After Fairburn Ings, the route is along a low magnesian limestone escarpment with a pleasant countryside of meadows and woodland, reminiscent of the Cotswolds. Fairburn, once a stagecoach stop on the Great North Road, and Ledsham, which has West Yorkshire's oldest church, are interesting and attractive villages. Some of the walk is only a few feet above sea level.

The **White Horse** is on the main street in the nearby village of Ledston. This popular pub, which is full of interesting local photographs, is over 200 years old. The menu includes a wide range of appetising dishes. Try the lamb and leek casserole or the red snapper. There are also curries and pasta, and a good value Sunday roast. The real ales are Black Sheep and Morland Old Speckled Hen.

The pub is open all day. Meals are served on Mondays and Tuesdays from 12 noon to 2.30 pm and 6 pm to 9.15 pm, Wednesdays 12 noon till 9 pm, Thursdays 11 am to 11 pm, Fridays and Saturdays 12 noon till 10 pm and Sundays 12 noon till 8 pm.
☎ *01977 533069*

Distance – 5 miles.

OS Explorer 289 Leeds. GR 453277.

Starting point The car park at the Fairburn Ings RSPB Reserve.

How to get there *Fairburn Ings Reserve is 3 miles north-east of Castleford. Turn off the M62 for Castleford at junction 31 or 32. Go north out of Castleford on the A656, then after just over a mile turn right at the traffic lights and continue for 2 miles to reach Fairburn Ings. For the White Horse take the first left after the lights. Check what time the car park closes, and allow at least 3 hours for the walk, longer if you intend to linger in the reserve. If you think there is insufficient time, park in Fairburn village near the information boards at point 2.*

West Yorkshire

1 From the car park, go to the **visitor centre**, which is well worth a look round. Follow the signs to **Pickup Hide**, then keep along the perimeter of the reserve, and follow the signs to the **Riverbank Trail**. Turn right through a kissing gate, then left along the Riverbank Trail. The **River Aire** can be glimpsed on the right, and you may see a barge. After ½ mile the path runs on a wooded bank between the river and the large lake on the left. Immediately after descending some steps, turn left along a path signposted to '**Cut Hide and village facilities**'. The crushed stone path follows the side of the lake on the left, and then leads into **Fairburn** (ignore all side paths), entering the village by **Well Trough Cottages** on **Cut Road**.

2 The two information boards are well worth a few minutes; they mention features of interest in the village, as well as describing the action of the nearby horse trough pump. Fairburn is on a limestone fault, which creates many natural springs; these were particularly valuable for watering the coaching horses in days gone by.

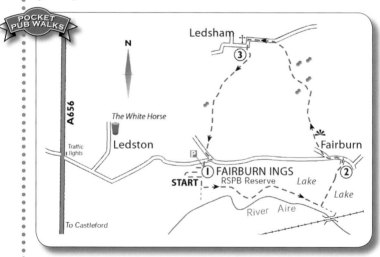

The lake at Fairburn Ings.

Turn left along the road for a short distance (though you may first wish to turn right to explore the village further), then right along **Beckfield Lane**. After 100 yards fork right on a lane that slants up the wooded escarpment and enters a field. There are views over to the **Pennines** and the **Emley Moor mast**. The clear path runs along the escarpment, and keeps to the left of the first two fields. In the third field follow the hedge on the right to a metal gate in the far corner. Slant left though woodland, continue in the same direction across a field, then bear right and along a broad track that goes just to the left of the wood. After 200 yards, the path goes over a stile (looks like a bit of fencing) into the wood and keeps close to the left-hand edge.

Keep in the same direction after the wood on a path that soon becomes a farm track with mature beeches on the left. When the road is reached, continue in the same direction into **Ledsham**, and go straight ahead on the path into the churchyard. The bottom part of Ledsham's church tower and the low doorway are Saxon, though the carvings round it are Victorian restoration. Inside the church are fine tombs, one of which belongs to Lady Mary Bolles whose ghost is said still to walk the village.

3 Leave the churchyard at the bottom left corner, cross the road and walk along **Newfield Lane**. Go left at the fork, past **High Meadows** and **White Gable**. Soon you are on an attractive farm lane (still Newfield Lane), part hedged, part open. The town in the distance is **Castleford**. After ½ mile the path enters a wood, and continues in the same direction keeping close to the side. Among the larger trees are some young elms; good luck to them. The path continues through woodland for over ½ mile, then drops to a road. The **RSPB Fairbairn Ings car park** is straight ahead.

For the **White Horse**, drive back along the **Castleford road**, then turn right to **Ledston** shortly before the traffic lights.

Places of interest nearby

Pontefract Castle, close to the centre of Pontefract, historically is one of England's great castles. Richard II died there. Not much of it survived the Civil War sieges, but this large and impressive site is well worth exploring. Admission free.

The New Inn

The undulated, well-wooded countryside to the south-east of Wakefield provides some enjoyable walking. This route goes through the grounds of Walton Hall, an early nature reserve (with a serious claim to be the world's first!) created by naturalist Charles Waterton. The walk, much of which is on the Waterton Trail, also visits the attractive large lake at Anglers Country Park, not long ago a deep opencast coal mine. Other features of the walk are the woodlands of Haw Park and the Barnsley Canal built in the 1790s, which, though now drained, has left a wooded ribbon winding through the countryside.

THE PUB The **New Inn** at Walton, probably a former canal pub, dates back to the 1700s. Now a popular village hostelry, it attracts visitors from further afield because of its good food. There is an extensive range of main courses, which can be eaten in the bar or in the restaurant. Try the home-cooked steak and kidney pie, or if you're lucky fresh sea bass will be on the specials. Real ales may include Caledonian Deuchars and Taylor's Landlord.

The pub is open all day, and the restaurant from 12 noon to 2 pm and 5 pm to 8.30 pm (Sundays 12 noon to 4 pm).
☎ *01924 255447*

[1] Turn left after leaving the **New Inn** then, after a few yards, turn right on a path marked '**Footpath and Pennine Trail**'. You are now on the filled-in bed of the **Barnsley Canal**, though you would hardly know. Just after the houses on the left, you pass the stone remains of a former lock; shortly after, turn left through a doorway in a high wall. This once went right round the **Waterton Estate**, and was built to keep the wildlife in and poachers out.

Distance – 5 miles

OS Explorer 278 Sheffield and Barnsley. GR 356172.

Starting point The New Inn at Walton.

How to get there *Walton is 3 miles south-east of Wakefield. Leave the M1 at junction 39, turn left along the A636, then turn right at the second roundabout along the A6186, following signs to Crofton. Turn left along the A61, then shortly afterwards along the B6132 and the B6378. Turn right at the T-junction at Greenside, then left along Shay Lane into Walton village. The New Inn is on the left. There is also a frequent bus service from Wakefield.*

2 Turn right along the wall and by the golf course putting green. Turn left when the road is reached, and keep to the fenced path. The path soon turns sharp left round a golf green, then through a gap in the wall on the right. Turn right shortly afterwards along an unmade road (signposted '**The Heronry, Waterton Trail**'), which then swings right with a golf fairway on the left. When the track divides, bear left and keep straight on, ignoring golf paths. Keep straight on at the wood. Do not turn right at the end of the lake, but follow the waymark sign and continue in the wood close to its edge on the left. Soon the path comes into the open and follows a ruined wall.

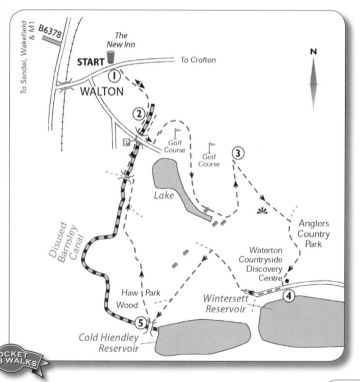

3 Cross the wall at a stile (where the field on the right comes to an end). Turn sharp right and slant across the field to a stile and footbridge. Keep by the hedge on the left in the next two fields to a stile where the fence bends right. Turn right along a track to soon arrive at the **Anglers Country Park lake.** The track soon leads out to the **Waterton Countryside Discovery Centre** which is well worth a visit.

4 Turn right along the lane at the back of the **Discovery Centre car park**. Go straight on at the metal gate, and continue along the lane to **Haw Park Wood**. Turn left just inside the wood on the track signposted to **Royston South** and go left shortly afterwards when it divides. Go straight on (by a post with a red circle) when the track swings right. The path soon reaches a junction of paths. On the left is a footbridge over the bed of the canal and beyond is **Cold Hiendley Reservoir** which fed the canal.

5 Turn sharp right along the woodland path to go past a seat with extravagantly carved ends (waymarked '**Trans Pennine Trail, Walton North**'). You soon leave the wood and continue on to join the side of the **Barnsley Canal** in a deep tree-lined cutting on the left. Turn left across the bridge, then immediately right on a path that soon joins the towpath. Go under a fine stone bridge (notice the rope markings) and continue along the canal to the **New Inn**.

Places of interest nearby

   Sandal Castle, just off the A61 one mile south of Wakefield, dates from Norman times. Although not much of the castle remains, it occupies a very attractive position, and there are good views westwards up the Calder valley. There is also a visitor centre.

10 Clayton West

Tilly's

The quality of the scenery near the southern boundary of West Yorkshire may surprise many people. This walk goes through pleasant meadowland, is always close to mature woodland, and has some excellent viewpoints. The jewel, however, is Bretton Country Park, not just an open-air sculpture park, but a mature and enjoyable example of large-scale landscape gardening. You can make it a whole day out by spending longer in the park, or taking a trip from Clayton West on the Kirklees Light Railway.

Distance – 6 miles.

OS Explorer 288 Bradford and Huddersfield and 278 Sheffield and Barnsley. GR 259109.

Starting point Tilly's at Clayton West.

How to get there *Clayton West is 8 miles south-west of Wakefield. Leave the M1 at junction 39 and take the A636 towards Denby Dale. After 6 miles, turn left along Long Lane at the Junction Inn, signposted 'Clayton West, High Hoyland'. Tilly's is on the left after a third of a mile. The moderately frequent Huddersfield to Barnsley bus service passes Tilly's.*

THE PUB

Tilly's is a pub restaurant with an attractive wide-ranging menu. Try the popular lamb shank kleftico braised with feta or the fried fillet of fresh turbot. Bar snacks are also available, and there is a traditional Sunday lunch, and a 2-course or 3-course Early Bird dinner with a good range of choices. The well-kept real ales at the time of writing were Copper Dragon and Acorn Regal.

Meals are available on Tuesdays to Fridays from 12.30 pm to 2.30 pm and 5.30 pm to 9.30 pm (closed Mondays), 4 pm to 9.30 pm on Saturdays and 2 pm to 7.30 pm on Sundays.
☎ *01484 865005*

1 Turn right for a few yards after leaving **Tilly's**, then turn right immediately after **Clayton Village Stores** along an enclosed path and into the attractive parkland of **Kayes Millennium Green**. Ignore the main path and bear slightly right on a level path to a kissing gate at the far end of the green. Turn right on a path that ascends the hillside by a wall on the right. Turn left

along the road at the top and when it turns left, keep straight on through a stile by a metal gate. Follow the path into a field, and keep by the wood on the left, then carry straight on to a stile at the top left-hand corner. In the next field keep to the left. Stay by the fence on the left in the following field, ignoring stiles on the left as you climb to a kissing gate. Cross a short belt of woodland, then slant left to another kissing gate at the top of **Winter Hill** (nearly 700 ft high).

2 Turn left and follow an attractive bridleway along the top of **Hoyland Bank** with woodland on the left. Turn left for a short distance when the path meets the road at a row of fine yew trees, and go past **High Hoyland church**. Turn right and follow the enclosed path round the edge of the churchyard, then keep straight on through a field to a junction of paths at a waymark

Bretton Hall seen from Cascade Bridge.

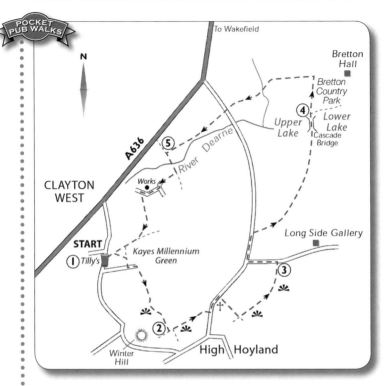

post. Turn left on a path, tree-lined at first, which leads through fields to **Jebb Lane**.

3 Turn left, then right at the road junction. Walk down the road for a short distance, then go over a stone step stile beside a gate and a house where there are kennels. Continue down the broad track through parkland with **Bretton Country Park** straight ahead. Just before the gate at the bottom, a ha-ha (sunken wall) is passed. Keep straight on to cross **Cascade Bridge**, which is a place to linger. There are attractive lakes on either side, plenty of birdlife, and a glimpse of **Bretton Hall** through the trees.

Immediately after the bridge, the delightful **Bretton Country Park** can be entered on the right.

4 Leave the park at the same point, and turn right and along a broad woodland track (i.e. go straight on after **Cascade Bridge**). After ¼ mile, turn left on a path signposted to **Clayton West**. The path stays close to a fence on the right, then carries on in the same direction across the field to a stile by the wall. Slant left down the hillside to a footbridge, then cross a field, keeping close to a fence on the right. Go straight on through a belt of woodland and cross the road to a stile. Now make for the far left-hand corner of a large meadow. The **River Dearne**, whose waters fill the Bretton Park lakes, is on the left. Go over two stiles in quick succession, then aim for the middle of the hedge at the far end of the field and cross a stile into a lane.

5 Turn left and follow the lane to a junction of lanes by the blue water treatment works notice. Turn right and continue along the lane to the end of a factory on the right. Go over the stile on the left by a gate, and continue on a clear path across fields. In the third field veer right to a stile by a tree, then cross another field to reach again the parkland of **Kayes Millennium Green**. Slant across the parkland to a kissing gate, then retrace your steps to **Tilly's**.

Places of interest nearby

Yorkshire Sculpture Park is well worth a visit, and it would be easy to spend an entire day there. In addition to the gardens and the sculpture park, there is an attractive walk up to Longside Gallery which has frequent exhibitions. The Sculpture Park is open daily free of charge, but there is a charge for car parking.
☎ *01924 832631.*

The Golden Cock

The route of this walk is through attractive woodlands and valleys, and there are many enjoyable views. However, the highlight of the circuit is Jubilee Tower, also known as Victoria Tower, which can be seen from the middle of Huddersfield and is a landmark for miles around. Castle Hill, on which it is situated, is a fine viewpoint and a place of considerable historic interest, having been the site of an Iron Age fort and later a Norman motte and bailey castle. Strangers to the area and perhaps some local residents will be surprised and delighted to find such tranquil rural countryside just to the south of Huddersfield.

Farnley Tyas (Walk 11

Distance – 4 miles.

OS Explorer 288 Bradford and Huddersfield. GR 165128.

Starting point The Golden Cock, Farnley Tyas.

How to get there *Farnley Tyas is 6 miles south-east of Huddersfield. Approaching from Huddersfield, take the A616, then immediately after the junction with the A6024 to Holmfirth, turn left to Honley Station and continue to Farnley Tyas. Or go by train, and join the walk at Honley Station (point 2).*

THE PUB The **Golden Cock** dates back at least to the early 1800s. Rent dinners used to be held here when tenant farmers from Farnley Tyas and the surrounding villages came to pay their rent to the nearby estate. Nowadays it is still a local pub, but patrons come from further afield to enjoy its good food and welcoming atmosphere. Try the braised steak with colcannon mash, Madeira and onion sauce, or the excellent three-course Sunday lunch with a wide range of choices. The real ales are Black Sheep, Taylor's and Tetley's.

Food is available from 12 noon to 3 pm on Monday to Saturday, 6 pm to 9 pm on Monday to Thursday, 6 pm to 9.30 pm on Friday and Saturday and 12 noon to 9 pm on Sunday.
☎ *01484 666644*

1 Turn right after leaving the **Golden Cock** and walk towards the church, then turn right down the road signposted to **Honley**. Less than ¼ mile after the junction and just after a 'Mud on Road' sign, turn left along a footpath, which keeps to the right of the field. It passes just to the left of the converted **Glen Farm** with good views across the **Holme Valley** to **Mag Dale** and the

Jubilee Tower.

saddleback hill called **Soldiers Lump**. The path descends, then goes through a stile and down steps to cross a stream (**Ludhill Dike**). Now flagged in places, the path keeps to the left side of a steep wooded valley, then maintains the same direction along a hillside close to the top of a field. It then descends through a wood. Veer slightly right at the end of the wood and cross a meadow to stepping stones over a stream. Turn sharp left immediately after the stream and go through a short stretch of woodland to an enclosed path between houses. Cross **Woodroyd Avenue**, continue along **Scop Royd Lane** and a narrow ginnel, then turn left under the railway bridge at **Honley Station**.

2 Turn right immediately into the former railway yard. After about 50 yards turn left into an enclosed path beside the yard. Turn right at the road to go uphill. When the road bends right, go up the enclosed footpath on the left (public footpath sign) then continue in the same direction up a field. There are good views and a convenient seat for pausing to appreciate them. Go to the right of a second seat (don't drop into woodland) and continue up the hillside on a clear path. After the path swings left in a long narrow field, **Jubilee Tower** comes into view.

3 At the road, turn briefly right, then left along a clear footpath on the left side of the field. Cross into the next field, now with the wall on the right. Stay on the path as it continues to the top of a

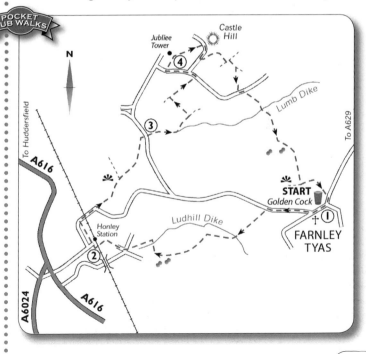

POCKET
PUB WALKS

steep wooded valley that drops down to the right, then go over a stile into a field and walk beside a wall on the left. Turn left at a stile halfway along the field, and keep beside the wall for two fields. Then turn right to a step stile and cross short fields to reach a road immediately to the left of a white house. Turn left, and at the top of the hill turn right and pant up the steep steps to the large stone tower looming above. **Jubilee Tower** was built by public subscription in 1897 to commemorate the 60th year of the reign of Queen Victoria.

4 Go across the grassed area to the road and, just after it bends right, turn sharp left at a footpath sign. This path leads into a field and then to a lane. Turn left, then, almost immediately, right and into a field. In the second field, slant right and follow the path towards the houses at **The Lumb**. The path, now enclosed, goes between two houses to an access road, and onto **Lumb Lane**. Turn left briefly, then right (public footpath sign). Now follow an attractive path that keeps more or less in the same direction for nearly a mile. It goes down fields into the **Lumb Dike** valley, then in woodland (up steps after the plank bridge), then into a meadow, then into woodland, then another short meadow, then woodland again (now climbing quite steeply), then up another meadow (climbing even more steeply). At the top left-hand corner of the field, the path leads into a pleasant enclosed lane, which swings left, then right to come out beside the **Golden Cock**.

Places of interest nearby

Huddersfield claims to have over 1,500 listed buildings. Of particular architectural note are the railway station which has a magnificent façade of Corinthian pillars, and the art gallery where you can see a painting by Francis Bacon and a Henry Moore sculpture.

12 **Holme**

The Fleece Inn

This fine walk in *Last of the Summer Wine* country is on paths that encircle the top end of the Holme Valley and there are ever-changing views of the nearby hills and moorland edges. The dominant hill is the dark presence of Black Hill (1,908 feet), West Yorkshire's highest peak. Another impressive feature is the deep gash of Ramsden Clough. The route of the walk does not go on the highest ground but keeps to the airy meadows of the hillsides. These are enclosed by a mosaic of dark stone walls; connoisseurs of stone stiles will have much to enthuse over! The reservoirs (there are four on the route) are a feature of the walk, and their shining waters and wooded shores do much to embellish the scene.

West Yorkshire

The **Fleece Inn** was once a livery stable for packhorses and is a welcoming little pub on the main road in Holme. The menu includes a popular home-made steak and ale pie, and I recently much enjoyed the Moroccan lamb dish. There are three real ales, Belhaven, Hook Norton and Banks's at the time of writing.

Meals are available from 12 noon to 2 pm on Tuesday to Saturday, 6 pm to 9 pm on Tuesday to Thursday, 6 pm to 9.30 pm on Friday and Saturday and 12 noon to 5 pm on Sunday. The Fleece is closed on Mondays.
☎ *01484 683449*

1 Turn left after leaving the **Fleece** and walk along the A6024 through this attractive village. Many of the stone houses were handloom weavers' cottages with large windows (by the standards of those days) to maximise the light. As you leave the village, go along a narrow lane on the right immediately after a cattle grid at the entrance to a house. Beyond the hedge on the right is a house with a turf roof. The lane leads to an enclosed path, which descends into the valley, first with the wall on the left, then on the right. Straight ahead, there are fine views of **Ramsden Clough** (access land and no longer private since

Distance – 5 miles.

OS Explorer 288 Bradford and Huddersfield. GR 107058.

Starting point The Fleece Inn at Holme.

How to get there *The small village of Holme is 3 miles south-west of Holmfirth on the A6024. There is a frequent bus service from Huddersfield.*

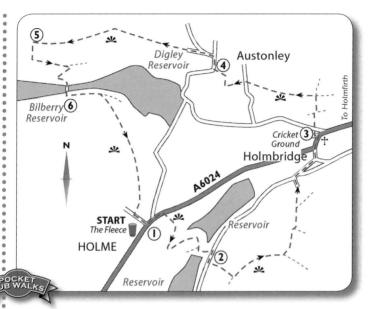

2004). The path veers right and enters a wood, then crosses a stream close to a waterfall. This is an enchanting spot. The wooded path climbs to the top of the valley, then swings right to drop into the next valley beside a line of metal railings. Ignore all paths to the right. Go on the path between the two reservoirs (**Brownhill** on the left, and **Ramsden** on the right), then turn right along the tarmac road at the top of the bank.

2 After a short distance, turn left at the footpath sign by the picnic site along a path that climbs by the left side of a wood. At the junction of paths, go straight ahead over the stile, then slant left on a clear path up the hillside. The path then follows a wall on the left. There are fine views into the **Holme Valley** (**Jubilee Tower** on **Castle Hill** can be seen in the distance), and back towards **Black Hill**. Shortly after a lane goes off on the left, go through a gated stile on the left. The path slants right at first, then

Fine views of Ramsden Clough can be enjoyed on the walk.

descends steeply by the left of a valley. It crosses the valley, goes through a gap in the wall and becomes an attractive wooded path down the side of the valley. Ignore the stile on the right and continue to the bottom of the wood. Cross a short field, admire the ducks, then go through two footpath gates immediately to the left of a house. Veer left down a tarmac lane, then turn right and down **Brownhill Lane** (ignore **Dobb Top Road**) to reach the main road again at **Holmbridge**. Keep straight on past the cricket ground and the church.

3 Immediately after the cricket ground, turn left up a flight of stone steps beneath a house. Cross a road, go between houses, cross another road and then climb up to a field. Turn right after the stile, then almost immediately afterwards, turn left up the hillside by a wall on the left. The path climbs two steep fields, then runs into a wide walled lane. Go over the stile on the left, keep to the wall on the left across three fields, then along a green lane. Cross the road to a stile beside the entrance to the stone hall opposite (**Austonley**). The path goes through a copse and keeps to the wall on the right when it enters a field. Go over the stone step stile on the right, and climb to the corner of the field by the wall on the left. Slant across the next field to a stile to the right of two gates, then down the steps to a tarmac road.

4 Turn right briefly, then left at the nearby road junction. Shortly afterwards (by 'No Parking') bear left along an unsurfaced walled lane which is followed for nearly a mile. It is level walking (for a change!) and there are fine views to the left throughout.

5 Shortly after a solitary sycamore, turn left down a walled lane on the left, which leads to a junction of tracks. Turn right on the track that descends into the valley, then sharp left through a metal gate and across the dam of **Bilberry Reservoir**. This was the scene of a terrible tragedy in 1852 when the dam, built to supply water to local mills, burst after days of heavy rain. The floods swept down the valley and killed 81 people.

6 After the dam, the clear path climbs the hillside and keeps fairly close to **Digley Reservoir** below. Watch out for a seat in memory of Ronald Pearson, and then two gates. Immediately after the second gate, cross a wide bridge over a small stream, then strike sharp right up a grassy bank. The bank soon leads to a clear path climbing the hillside to a wooden step stile. After this, the path continues in more or less the same direction across several fields, climbing gently towards **Holme**. There are good views to the left with **Ramsden Clough** again prominent. The path eventually leads into a walled green lane, which comes out onto a tarmac road. Turn left down the road into **Holme village**, then at the bottom turn right to the **Fleece**.

Places of interest nearby

Holmfirth is a pleasant and lively small town. It is now best known as the location for the TV series *Last of the Summer Wine*, where Sid's Café, Nora Batty's steps, and other familiar scenes can conveniently be visited. Nearly all of Britain's 'naughty' seaside postcards were produced in Holmfirth, and there is now a postcard museum.

13 Triangle

The Millbank

This walk visits the **Ryburn Valley,** and provides an excellent illustration of the enjoyable countryside that can be found in West Yorkshire very close to the towns. From some of the route you can look down into Sowerby Bridge and across to Halifax, but you will also find deep woodland, airy hillsides, moorland, old walled lanes and flagged paths (keep walking them – they are grassing over!). And there are lots of interesting views.

THE PUB The **Millbank** is in the hillside hamlet of Mill Bank. Turn south-west off the A58 at Triangle and the pub is on the left after two-thirds of a mile. It looks like a row of cottages – as indeed it was! On a fine day have a meal or drink at the back and enjoy the view across the valley. The Millbank has

> **Distance** – 6 miles.
>
> **OS Explorer** Outdoor Leisure 21 South Pennines.
> GR 043221.
>
> **Starting point** The junction of the A58 and Stansted Mill Lane at Triangle, near the Triangle pub. Park on the A58, which is quite wide, or near the bottom of the lane to Mill Bank. (Parking on Stansted Mill Lane is not advised.)
>
> ***How to get there*** *Triangle is on the A58, just over a mile from Sowerby Bridge and 4 miles south-west of Halifax. Public transport users can take the train to Sowerby Bridge (good services from Leeds and Bradford), and one of the frequent buses along the A58.*

a deservedly popular local restaurant with an extensive menu. Try the ravioli of Scottish lobster with vegetable broth, or roast suckling pig. There is also an attractive two courses and coffee menu. The well-looked-after real ales are Tetley's and Taylor's.

Food is available at lunchtime from 12 noon to 2.30 pm on Tuesday to Saturday and 12 noon to 4.30 pm on Sunday. In the evening the times are 6 pm to 9.30 pm on Monday to Thursday, 6 pm to 10 pm on Friday and Saturday and 6 pm to 8 pm on Sunday.
☎ 01422 825588

1 A few yards on the **Sowerby Bridge** side of the junction where the lane to the **Millbank pub** goes off the A58, turn right on '**Stansted Mill Lane Leading to Grassy Bottoms**'. The lane leads steeply down to the valley bottom, crosses the **River Ryburn** and goes past the ground of **Triangle Cricket Club**

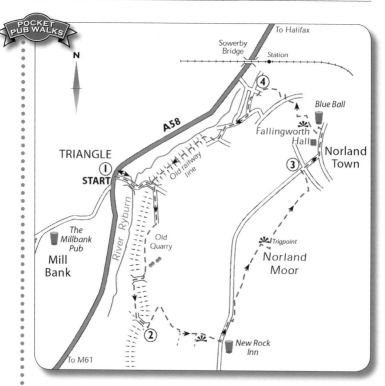

POCKET
PUB WALKS

To Halifax

Sowerby
Bridge

Station

N

Blue Ball

A58

Fallingworth
Hall

TRIANGLE

① START

Old railway
line

③

Norland
Town

River Ryburn

The
Millbank
Pub

Old
Quarry

Mill
Bank

Trigpoint

Norland
Moor

②

To M61

New Rock
Inn

(surely one of the most attractive cricket grounds in the land).
After going over the bridge of the former railway branch line
to Ripponden, turn right along a narrow tarmac lane. Keep
straight on past houses on the left and a potting shed on the
right and continue along a footpath at the edge of a wood. The
path becomes less distinct, but it keeps going in more or less the
same direction along the valley; it crosses a gully and then fords
a tributary stream before coming out at a bridge over the former
railway. Cross the bridge, keep on a wooded path close to the
railway (in a deep chasm on the left), then cross the line again
on another solid stone bridge.

2 Turn sharp left on a track signposted to **Scammonden Road**. Go to the right of a house (waymark), then almost immediately turn right and ascend the hillside on an attractive walled path. This swings left then right. Ignore the path on the right to **Ripponden Old Bank**. After the path leaves the woodland, there are fine views over **Ripponden** to the **Pennine hills** beyond. Continue up the lane, which passes houses and comes out on a road at the **New Rock Inn**. Turn left along the road for a short distance, then go along the moorland path close to the right of the road. Continue along the **Calderdale Way** path over **Norland Moor** and past a prominent rock to reach the trig point. There are good views to the left across the **Ryburn Valley** and extensive views eastwards (**Ferrybridge Power Station** can easily be seen). Turn left at the trig point and continue on a broad moorland path in the direction of the octagonal **Wainhouse Tower** on the skyline. This is 253 feet high and was formerly the chimney of a dye-works. Fine views continue, particularly to the left up **Calderdale.** Just before the moor ends, turn left by a line of wooden pylons to a children's playground, then turn right when the road is reached.

3 Carry straight on at the crossroads past the school, then left at the T-junction onto **Norland Town Road**. You will pass **Fallingworth Hall**, an attractive stone building dating from 1642, on the left. Almost immediately afterwards, turn left down the side of the **Blue Ball pub** on a footpath signposted to **Allan Park**. Keep to the left side of the wall, then when a line

Looking towards Calderdale from near point 3.

of standing stones is reached, strike across the field to a stile at the bottom left-hand corner. In the next field, follow the wall on the right to a stile near the left-hand corner, then follow the flagged path to a narrow tarmac road. Briefly turn left, then right immediately after the house and caravan (the path is easy to miss) down a narrow walled lane. You are almost on top of **Sowerby Bridge railway station**, deep below on the right. The path leads to a terrace of stone houses.

2 Turn left immediately after the terrace (but right if you want a direct route into **Sowerby Bridge**) for a few yards, then go right on an unmade road between garages. Turn left at the end and go up **Boggart Lane** (steep, but not much of it!), then turn right at the top. Continue down the tarmac road and keep straight on at the road junction. Bear left at the next road junction onto **Long Lane** (cul de sac sign). When it bends sharp left, take the footpath on the right, which leads down to the former railway line to Ripponden. Turn left along the permissive path along the line and continue for about ½ mile. It is attractive, wooded walking, very shaded when the leaves are fully out. When the path swings left in a deep cutting, slant right on a path that climbs the bank, then runs along the top. Below is the cricket ground, and your steps can be retraced to where the walk started.

Places of interest nearby

Halifax is perhaps best known for its building society, now Halifax PLC, but for centuries it was an important centre of the cloth trade. The Piece Hall, an 18th-century cloth market, is an impressive and unique building. The 15th-century parish church has fine Perpendicular architecture and the giant gargoyles are but one of many features of interest.

14 Hebden Bridge

The Stubbing Wharf

You won't find **Jumble Hole on the map,** it's Delph. But whatever it's called, it's a fine wooded valley and a walker's delight. And so is the spectacular Colden Clough, the next valley along. Then up on the hill there's Heptonstall, one of the most interesting villages in Yorkshire. And here's nothing quite like Hebden Bridge. Unusual four-storey terrace housing clinging to the steep hillsides gives the town a unique appearance, and right in the busy town centre is an ancient packhorse bridge. Several parts of the walk are on stone flagged paths called causeways, much used in the days when packhorses or Shanks's pony were more convenient than the wheel. This is one of the best half-day walks you'll find anywhere.

Distance – 6 miles.

OS Explorer Outdoor Leisure 21 South Pennines.
GR 985272.

Starting point The Stubbing Wharf pub, Hebden Bridge.

How to get there The Stubbing Wharf pub is ½ mile west of Hebden Bridge, just off the A646 between Halifax and Todmorden. Approaching westwards along the valley from Halifax, turn left to the Stubbing Wharf, immediately after the Heptonstall turning circle. Hebden Bridge has a frequent rail service from Leeds, Bradford and Halifax.

THE PUB The **Stubbing Wharf** backs onto Rochdale Canal in an attractive setting. It is a popular pub, particularly for those who like real ales, and Caledonian Deuchars, Black Sheep, Taylor's Landlord, Flowers and a guest beer are on offer. A good selection of food is also served. Try the Cajun chicken with chips and peas, the steaks or the large mixed grill.

Food is available from 12 noon till 2.30 pm and 5 pm to 8.30 pm, excluding Sunday evening.
☎ *01422 844107*

1 Leave the **Stubbing Wharf** pub by the back door, and climb to the towpath of the **Rochdale Canal.** Turn right and follow the attractive path for two-thirds of a mile. On the left after the railway bridge is a steep wooded hillside and on the right the **River Calder**. This canal was the first of the three trans-Pennine canals to be completed and the full length between Sowerby Bridge and Manchester was opened in 1804.

2 Turn right when you reach the stone bridge over the canal and follow the **Pennine Way**, which turns right when it reaches the A646, then shortly afterwards turns left under the railway bridge. Keep with the Pennine Way as it ascends steeply on a cobbled walled path. Just before a house on the left, turn left through a gated stile (easy to miss) and into a field. Slant right in the second field and follow a fence to reach an access road. Turn left down the road past an old chimney and into **Jumble Clough** ('**Delph**' on the map). Keep to the unmade road as it climbs the valley. Follow the road when it crosses the stream and turns sharp right to continue up the valley. When the lane turns left, keep straight on along an enjoyable woodland path. Ignore side paths, and after a mile you pass an old mill. Cross the stream on a footbridge and climb up to a meadow.

3 Turn left at the footpath signpost and keep the wall on your right. Turn right after a gate stile at **Hippins** and follow the path (now the **Calderdale Way**) as it gently climbs the hillside past scattered housing. The path swings right at the top of a

Heptonstall's ruined church.

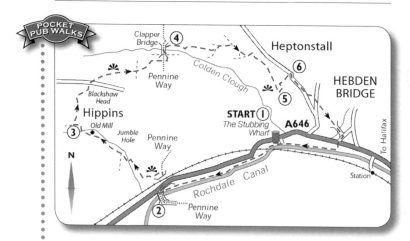

field and becomes enclosed, then goes through a metal gate by the left of a house to reach the road at **Blackshaw Head**. Go right for a few yards, then through a stile on the left. The path slants across the field and continues in the same direction across several fields. It crosses a lane (go left for a few yards) and joins another lane immediately after going round a house. Turn right, and then left at a crossing of paths by a metal gate. The path (the **Pennine Way** again) descends steeply into the valley and crosses the stream on a magnificent stone clapper bridge.

4 Continue on the stone path up the hillside to a junction of paths by a footpath post, where you leave the **Pennine Way** and bear right along an attractive flagged path (still the **Calderdale Way**). Go over the stile into the field (ignore the path that keeps in the wood) and continue in the same direction through several fields. Bear left when the path joins a lane and soon after turn right by the left side of a house. At a junction of paths by a pine tree, bear slightly right and keep a wall on the left. Turn left for a short distance up a lane, then at a footpath sign turn right and into a wood. Shortly afterwards, turn left at a footpath post and keep close to the top of the wood on a rocky route which is almost a scramble at times. The path then keeps to the rocky edge of **Colden Clough** with fine views across the valley.

5 Turn left into **Heptonstall** along a walled path with houses on either side. Just before the church, turn left along the wall round the churchyard. In the newer graveyard on the left is the grave of the poet Sylvia Plath, an insignificant monument, not easily found (though, as a clue, it is over the far side). Now take the path that goes round the left of the church and enjoy the surprise of seeing the older church, now ruined, round the corner. Go to its right, past the former grammar school (now a museum) and on to the main street. Turn left past **Weavers Square** to the top of the village and see some of the weavers' cottages (those with the large windows at the top), then retrace your steps and keep straight on down Towngate.

6 Continue down Towngate and out of **Heptonstall**. After a few hundred yards, turn left down a path with a handrail, and descend steps to another road. Turn right for a short distance, then go down a steep cobbled lane marked 'Unsuitable for Motors'. Keep straight on across the packhorse bridge ('erected c1510 AD', see noticeboard) when **Hebden Bridge** is reached. Turn right after the bridge, then go straight across at the traffic lights along **Holme Street**, past the post office and trades club. When you come to the canal, turn right along the towpath and on a fine stone aqueduct over the **Calder**. The **Stubbing Wharf** is ½ mile ahead.

Places of interest nearby

Hardcastle Crags, owned by the National Trust, is a splendid wooded valley. While the crags themselves are not particularly impressive, the woods and the fast-flowing stream are a delight.

The Top Brink Inn

This walk is cram-full of interest. There is the architecture and wildlife of the Rochdale Canal, the attractive town of Todmorden, old packhorse paths, the village of Mankinholes and the old mill at Lumbutts. There are many fine views, particularly across Calderdale from Langfield Common. The long climb out of Todmorden, steep in places, may cause some perspiration. The good news is that it is virtually the only climb.

THE PUB The **Top Brink Inn** at Lumbutts overlooks Langfield Edge. It is a popular pub and offers a wide range of food. Try the three 4oz lamp chops with mint sauce, or the fillet of beef stroganoff. There are also blackboard specials. The real ales are Boddington's, Taylor's Landlord, Castle Eden and Flowers

Original, plus a guest beer. The pub is attractively decorated and there are lots of shining horse brasses.

Meals are available on weekdays from 12 noon to 2.30 pm (not Mondays and Tuesdays) and 6 pm to 10 pm; 12 noon to 10 pm on Saturdays and Sundays.
☎ *01706 812696*

1 Go along a walled lane between the houses at the far end of the pub car park. Keep by the wall on the left in the first field, and then along an enclosed path. Turn sharp right after the stile (signposted '**Calderdale Way Link Path**') on a path that clings to a steep hillside, before descending to an enclosed path by a wire fence. Keep straight on when the path comes to a lane, then turn right when a tarmac road is reached.

2 Immediately after the **Rochdale Canal** is crossed at **Woodhouse Mill** (now apartments), go down the steps on the right, then turn

> **Distance** – 6½ miles.
>
> **OS Explorer** Outdoor Leisure 21 South Pennines. GR 956235.
>
> **Starting point** The Top Brink Inn at Lumbutts.
>
> **How to get there** *Take the A646 between Hebden Bridge and Todmorden. Approaching from the east, ignore the first turn to Lumbutts (which has a wicked hairpin bend) and take the next one. Turn left at the T-junction, then soon turn sharp left to the Top Brink. Todmorden has a good rail service from Leeds, Bradford and Halifax, and the walk can easily be joined at Todmorden town hall, close to the station.*

right again along the towpath under the bridge. Continue along the towpath towards **Todmorden**. It is enjoyable level walking, with a canal milepost (**Sowerby Bridge 9 miles, Manchester 23 miles**), attractive locks, bridges and overflow channels. There are barges (nearly always moored), anglers and plenty of birdlife. After its decline and closure, the canal became a weed-ridden dumping ground. Its restoration is a recreational triumph.

3 After a mile, leave the canal at a display board about **Todmorden**, and follow the sign to '**Markets'**. Todmorden is a town of character and charm. The Fielden family, local millowners in the 1800s, were responsible for most of the significant buildings, including the town hall and Unitarian church. Turn left up the main road to the central road junction. Straight ahead is the diminutive parish church. On the right is a gem of a town hall: particularly notice the carving round the top. Beyond the town hall, the railway viaduct is worth a glance. Now turn left along **Rochdale Road** as far as the canal (recognisable by a bulge in the road), to make a brief detour to see **The Great Wall Of Tod**; turn right and walk along the towpath till you reach the corner, at which point you can gawp at a gigantic brick canal wall. Return to **Rochdale Road** and continue for a few yards to **Fielden Square** (actually a triangle).

4 Leave the square by **Honey Hole Lane**. Ahead is the Unitarian church, a Grade 1 listed building. Go past **Well Street**, then sharp right up the steeply climbing **Shoebroad Lane**. Keep straight on past the houses and into open country, still climbing. When the lane bends left and becomes level, take the path straight ahead, which goes up the left side of a field. The path crosses a road, and now signposted '**Gaddings Dam**' makes for the left of the house ahead, which it skirts by an enclosed path. Then turn left up the walled path to the gate onto the moor (**Langfield Common**).

5 Bear right on a path that gradually swings left as it climbs the hillside, and carry straight on at a waymark post. When the path

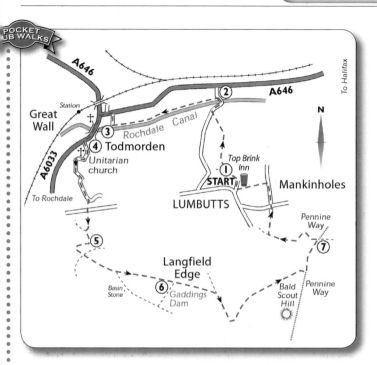

leaves a shallow rocky channel and bears right towards a post on the near horizon, take a faint path that carries straight on up the moor. **Stoodley Pike monument** looms up in the distance. The path, always fairly straight, goes to the left corner of the grassy bank ahead and then climbs steps up to **Gaddings Dam**.

6 Keep straight on with the dam on the right, followed by a drained dam. Continue in the same direction (the path is narrow, but clear) to **Langfield Edge** on the left. Ignore a path that turns off sharply to the left and, soon afterwards, cross (boggy bits) the headwaters of two streams descending into the nearby valley. The path then keeps to the top of the hillside with good views into **Calderdale**, and crosses **Bald Scout Hill** close to a helpful cairn.

Note that the latter section of this path does not follow the right of way; however, it can be legitimately walked as this is Access Land. Turn left when the path joins the **Pennine Way** (a good mile after **Gaddings Dam**) and follow it to a crossroads of paths.

7 Turn left down the paved packhorse path into the valley below, probably the

Going down the paved path towards Mankinholes.

best paved path in the Pennines. A further bonus is that you are going down. Turn right at the gate at the bottom, and follow a walled lane into **Mankinholes**. Notice the splendid horse troughs on the right, and the handloom weavers' cottages. Turn left by a footpath sign immediately after the youth hostel, and follow the path down the field to the **Top Brink**. The tall stone building that looks like an enlarged version of an early mobile phone is **Lumbutts Mill**, which once housed three water wheels. For a closer look, go down the steps from the pub car park.

Places of interest nearby

The walk can be extended at point 7 to include a visit to **Stoodley Pike monument** on the far end of the hillside. You can climb the dark stairway to the viewing gallery, where there is a good prospect of Calderdale and the surrounding hills (though it isn't a deal more impressive than if you had stayed at the bottom). The monument was built in 1856; its predecessor, erected to mark the end of the Napoleonic Wars, unfortunately collapsed.